Understanding Coding Using

BOOLEAN LOGIC

Patricia Harris

PowerKiDS
press™

New York

Published in 2017 by The Rosen Publishing Group, Inc.
29 East 21st Street, New York, NY 10010

Copyright © 2017 by The Rosen Publishing Group, Inc.

First Edition

Editor: Greg Roza
Book Design: Michael J. Flynn

Photo Credits: Cover uniquely india/Getty Images; cover, pp. 1, 3–24 (coding background) Lukas Rs/Shutterstock.com; p. 5 Print Collector/Hulton Archive/Getty Images; p. 9 https://en.wikipedia.org/wiki/File:Cowardly_lion2.jpg; p. 11 Silver Screen Collection/Moviepix/Getty Images; p. 12 (relay) Abraksis/Shutterstock.com; p. 12 (diode) Preobrajenskiy/Shutterstock.com; p. 12 (transistor) airobody/Shutterstock.com; p. 13 Volodymyr Krasyuk/Shutterstock.com; p. 15 Rawpixel.com/Shutterstock.com; p. 19 BartCo/E+/Getty Images; p. 21 Radovan1/Shutterstock.com.

Cataloging-in-Publication Data

Names: Harris, Patricia.
Title: Understanding coding using boolean logic / Patricia Harris.
Description: New York : PowerKids Press, 2017. | Series: Spotlight on kids can code | Includes index.
Identifiers: ISBN 9781499428063 (pbk.) | ISBN 9781499428162 (library bound) | ISBN 9781499428841 (6 pack)
Subjects: LCSH: Computer programming–Juvenile literature. | Electronic information resource searching–Juvenile literature. | Algebra, Boolean.
Classification: LCC QA76.52 H37 2017 | DDC 005.1–dc23

Manufactured in the United States of America

CPSIA Compliance Information: Batch #BW17PK: For Further Information contact Rosen Publishing, New York, New York at 1-800-237-9932

Contents

Meet George Boole

George Boole grew up in England in the early 1800s. His family wasn't rich, and he didn't receive much formal education. He learned mathematics from his father and the Greek language from a friend of his father. Boole taught himself Latin. By the time he was 16 years old, he had become an assistant teacher. At 20, he opened his own school and taught mathematics. He eventually became a college professor of mathematics.

Boole's work in **logic** began at a time when there were arguments about that topic. Boole didn't want to set aside Aristotle's traditional logic. Rather, he wanted to extend logic into mathematics. His book, *An Investigation into the Laws of Thought, on Which are Founded the Mathematical Theories of Logic and* **Probabilities**, described his ideas.

Aristotle's Logic

Aristotle was a Greek philosopher who lived from 384 to 322 BC. He's believed to be the first great thinker to explore and write about the topic of logic. Aristotle's writings formed the core of Western logic up until the 19th century.

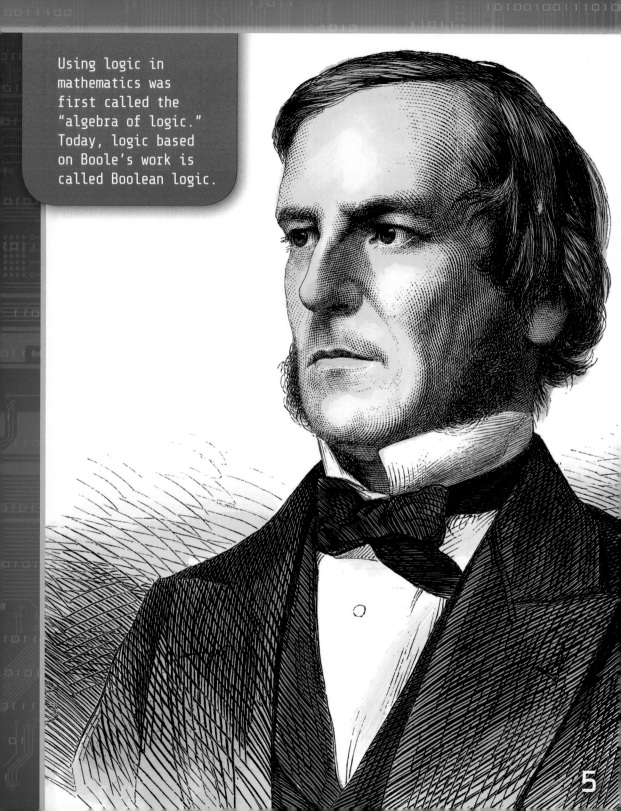

Using logic in mathematics was first called the "algebra of logic." Today, logic based on Boole's work is called Boolean logic.

The Need for Boolean Logic

In the 1930s, American college student Claude Shannon learned about Boole's work. He wrote a **master's thesis** on how Boolean algebra could be used with electrical switches to solve problems. Many years later, people used Boolean logic as the foundation for digital **circuit** design. Boolean logic became the foundation for the creation of computers.

Boolean logic is used in programming. It uses special connectors—such as AND, OR, and NOT—to allow programs to function. The search engine Google assumes you want to use an AND connector. Searching for "transportation" on Google returns information on many kinds of transportation. Searching for "transportation *and* trains" gives us mostly information on trains. However, Google isn't very good at NOT connectors.

Google | transportation and trains

All　News　Images　Videos　Maps　More ▾　Search tools

About 124,000,000 results (0.60 seconds)

Amtrak: Train & Bus Tickets - National Railroad - USA & Canada
https://www.amtrak.com/ ▾ Amtrak ▾
Get your **train** and bus tickets or other Thruway services on Amtrak.com to travel over 500 destinations
via 30 plus **train** routes in the USA and Canada.
Amtrak Train Schedules - Routes & Stations - Deals - Contact Us

New York Museum of Transportation
4.3 ★★★★☆ (6) · Museum
6393 E River Rd · (585) 371-5797
Closed today
　　　　　Website　Directions

US Federal Railroad Administration
No reviews · Federal Government Office
　　　　　Website　Directions

Searching the Internet for information is easier with Boolean logic. It helps pinpoint the types of websites you want to see.

Google | transportation NOT trains

All　Images　News　Videos　Shopping　More ▾　Search tools

About 123,000,000 results (0.59 seconds)

Images for transportation NOT trains　　　　　Report images

More images for transportation NOT trains

MTA | Subway, Bus, Long Island Rail Road, Metro-North
www.mta.info/ ▾ Metropolitan Transportation Authority ▾
Plan Your Trip to JFK and LGA by Subway, Bus and **Train** ... Plan will renew, enhance and expand our
transportation network with a $29.5 billion investment ...

Rail transport - Wikipedia, the free encyclopedia
https://en.wikipedia.org/wiki/Rail_**transport** ▾ Wikipedia ▾
Jump to Passenger **trains** - Passenger **trains** are part of public **transport** and often make up ... intercity
trains but the speeds are **not** as high as those in the ...
History of rail transport - Glossary of rail transport terms - Rail transport by country

Rail freight transport - Wikipedia, the free encyclopedia
https://en.wikipedia.org/wiki/Rail_freight_**transport** ▾ Wikipedia ▾
Rail freight **transport** is the use of railroads and **trains** to **transport** cargo as opposed to human ....
Freight **trains** are sometimes illegally boarded by individuals who do **not** wish, or do **not** have the ...

Lions and Tigers and Bears!

The movie *The Wizard of Oz* has a well-known scene in which Dorothy's new friends warn her about scary things she might meet in the new land. Dorothy asks about wild animals in the forest. The answer she gets leads to the famous line "Lions and tigers and bears! Oh, my!" The line means that Dorothy is worried she will meet all of these animals in the forest.

The word "and" is a conjunction that joins words and topics together. We love to eat spaghetti and meatballs, peanut butter and jelly, and macaroni and cheese. In Dorothy's case, we don't expect her to meet all three animals at once. However, if we applied Boolean logic to this famous movie line, she definitely would have met all three!

Shortly after the scene described here, Dorothy meets the Cowardly Lion. She does not see tigers and bears.

"*You ought to be ashamed of yourself!*"

What happens in *The Wizard of Oz* is what we would expect using traditional logic. We read the "and" but don't think Dorothy must meet all the animals together. With Boolean logic, however, the statement "lions and tigers and bears" joins the three animals using the connector "and." That means all three animals need to show up for the statement to be true.

We can use Boolean logic to make the movie line more exact. We need to use another common connector— "or." Like "and," "or" is a conjunction. However, "or" separates items instead of joining them. Changing the line to "lions or tigers or bears" means Dorothy will bump into just one of those animals, not all three. That's exactly what happens!

"Lions and tigers and bears! Oh, my!"

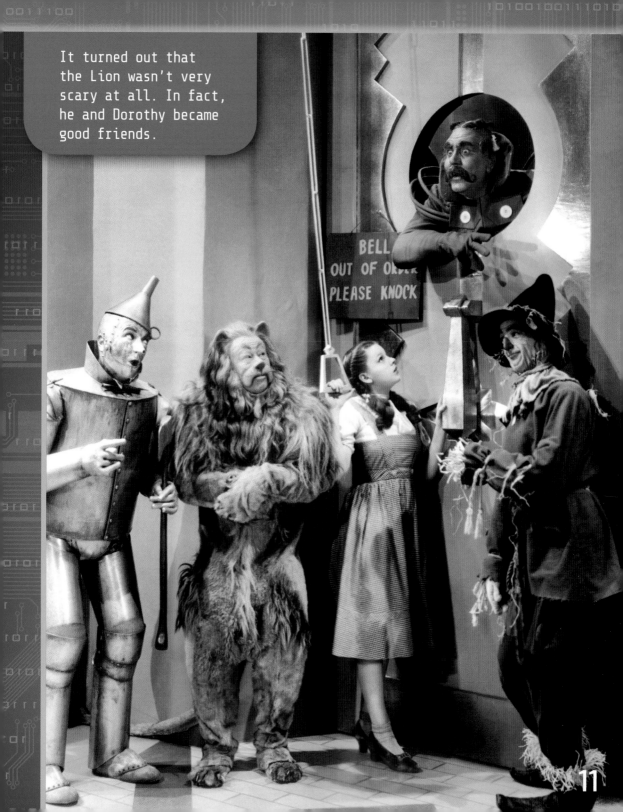

It turned out that the Lion wasn't very scary at all. In fact, he and Dorothy became good friends.

Through the Gate

Claude Shannon worked to apply Boolean logic to electrically driven **mechanical** switches. He used his ideas to make the switches in a telephone system work better. Russian mathematicians, especially Victor Shestakov, also worked to apply Boolean logic to electric switches. Shannon and Shestakov did not work with digital circuits. However, their work provided a foundation for the design of digital circuits and the beginning of modern-day computers.

Digital circuits are made up of electronic **components** that act as switches. They require logic gates to work properly. A logic gate in a computer is a physical device such as a **diode**, **transistor**, or **relay**. In computers, transistors are often used for the gates.

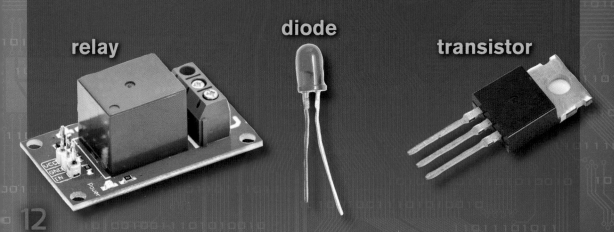

relay

diode

transistor

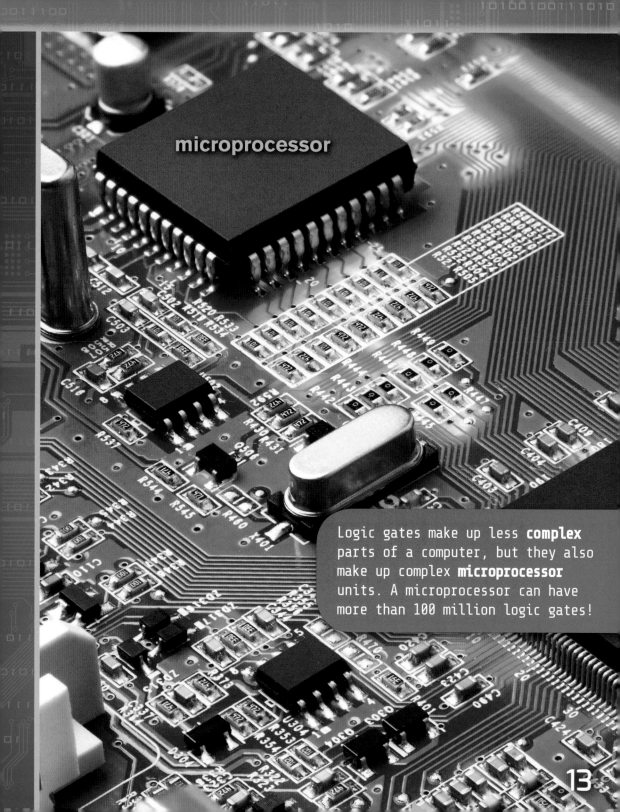

microprocessor

Logic gates make up less **complex** parts of a computer, but they also make up complex **microprocessor** units. A microprocessor can have more than 100 million logic gates!

AND and OR Gates

In computers, logic gates let information pass from an input to an output in different ways. The most common gates are AND gates, OR gates, and NOT gates. The AND gate is much like the use of "and" in a sentence. Think of the sentence "José and Sarah always eat their vegetables." The word "and" joins the two people. This sentence means that eating vegetables is "true" for both children.

The AND gate circuit will have two or more logic gate connections in the circuit. In Boolean logic, both connections of an AND gate must be turned on for the gate to work. All gates must return a "true" or "on" state for the circuit to make the output "true" or "on."

Input/Output

We use computers every day. We give them a task to do, and then we receive a response. The task we give computers is called "input," and the response is called "output." For example, when you're playing a video game on a computer, the keyboard and mouse allow you to input information. When you see your game character move based on your input, that's called output.

The **schematic** for an AND gate looks like this. If AND gates are linked to pass information through to new AND gates, all the information must be "true" or "on" for the final output to be "on." In this diagram the combined circuit is off even though two of the three gates are on.

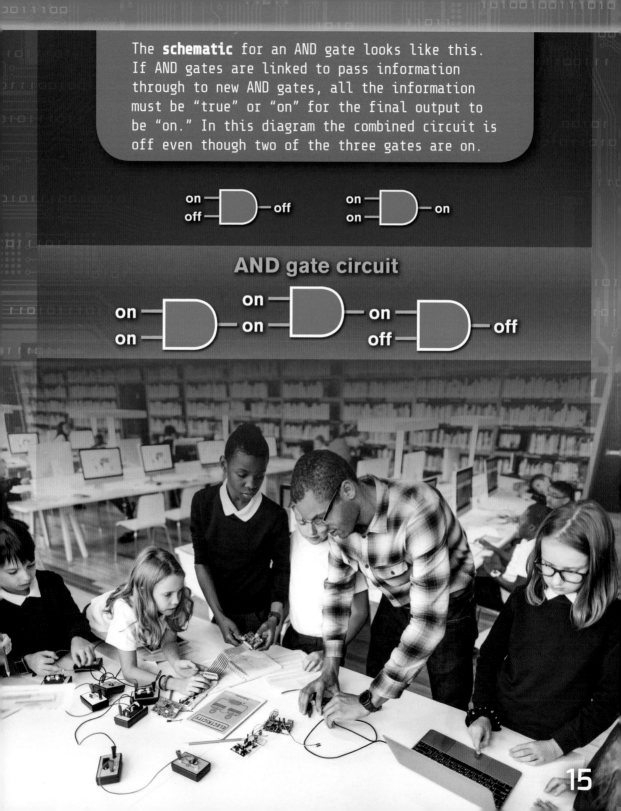

on — off
off

on — on
on

AND gate circuit

on — on

on — on

on — off

Think back to *The Wizard of Oz*. If Dorothy's statement uses Boolean logic, "and" means that meeting all of those animals would be scary. Boolean logic applies the same way to circuits. Using Boolean logic, both of the inputs to the gate must be "on" for the output to be "on."

OR gates work just like the word "or." In Boolean logic, for Dorothy to be afraid of just one of the animals, the sentence would have to be "Lions or tigers or bears." In computer circuitry, the OR gate means that the circuit returns a "true" or "on" state if one or more of the gates are "true" or "on." It only returns a "false" or "off" output if both the gates are "off."

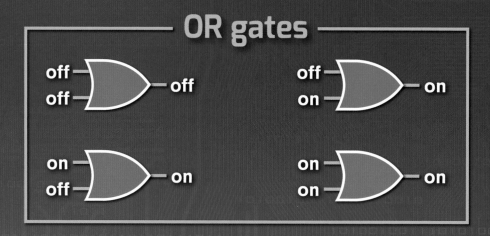

OR gates

off
off — off

off
on — on

on
off — on

on
on — on

This is a simple AND gate circuit with two switches. Notice that the light only works when both switches are closed, or "on."

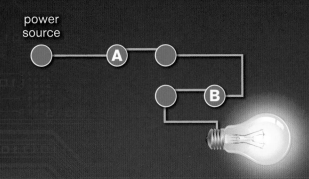

power
source

**A switch closed (on)
B switch closed (on)**

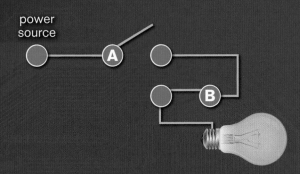

power
source

**A switch open (off)
B switch closed (on)**

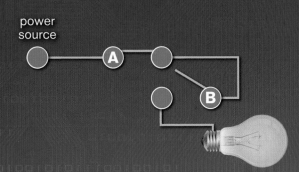

power
source

**A switch closed (on)
B switch open (off)**

NOT and NAND Gates

NOT logic gates are interesting logic gates. They're called inverters, and they change how a switch works. A "true" or "on" switch becomes a "false" or "off" switch and a "false" or "off" switch becomes a "true" or "on" switch. The NOT gate is like the "not" in the sentence "Sarah does not eat her vegetables." And what a shame because she may miss out on dessert! For the NOT gate the information comes in as one state and goes out as the opposite state.

The NAND gate is a NOT gate linked to an AND gate. So if both the inputs are "on," the output is "off." If only one input or neither input is "on," the output is "on." That is the opposite of an AND gate!

NAND gates

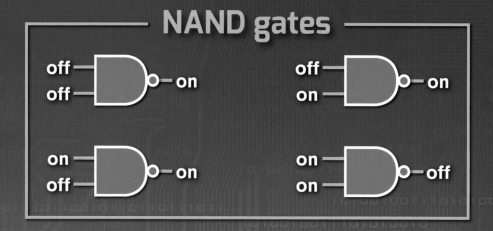

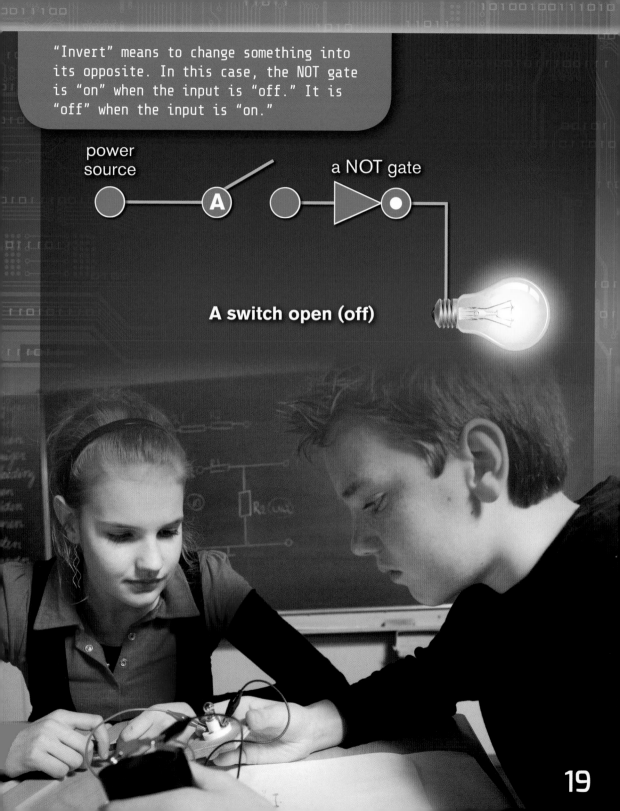

"Invert" means to change something into its opposite. In this case, the NOT gate is "on" when the input is "off." It is "off" when the input is "on."

power source

a NOT gate

A

A switch open (off)

19

NOR, XOR, and XNOR Gates

The NOR gate is like an OR gate followed by a NOT gate. So if both inputs are "off," the output is "on." If one or both of the inputs are "on," the output is "off."

The XOR gate is an **exclusive** OR gate. In Boolean logic the OR gate means that the circuit returns an "on" or "true" state if one or more of the gates are "true." The use of XOR means that the OR output is "true" when only one of the inputs is "true." It returns a "false" if both the inputs are "true" or "false." One can think of this gate as an "either/or" logic choice.

The XNOR gate is an exclusive NOR gate. It really is an XOR followed by a NOT. If both inputs are the same, the output is "true." If the inputs are different, the output is "false."

NOR gate | XOR gate | XNOR gate

Computers rely on binary code, shown here, to function. A "0" stands for off, and "1" stands for on. Combinations of these numbers are used to give instructions to computers.

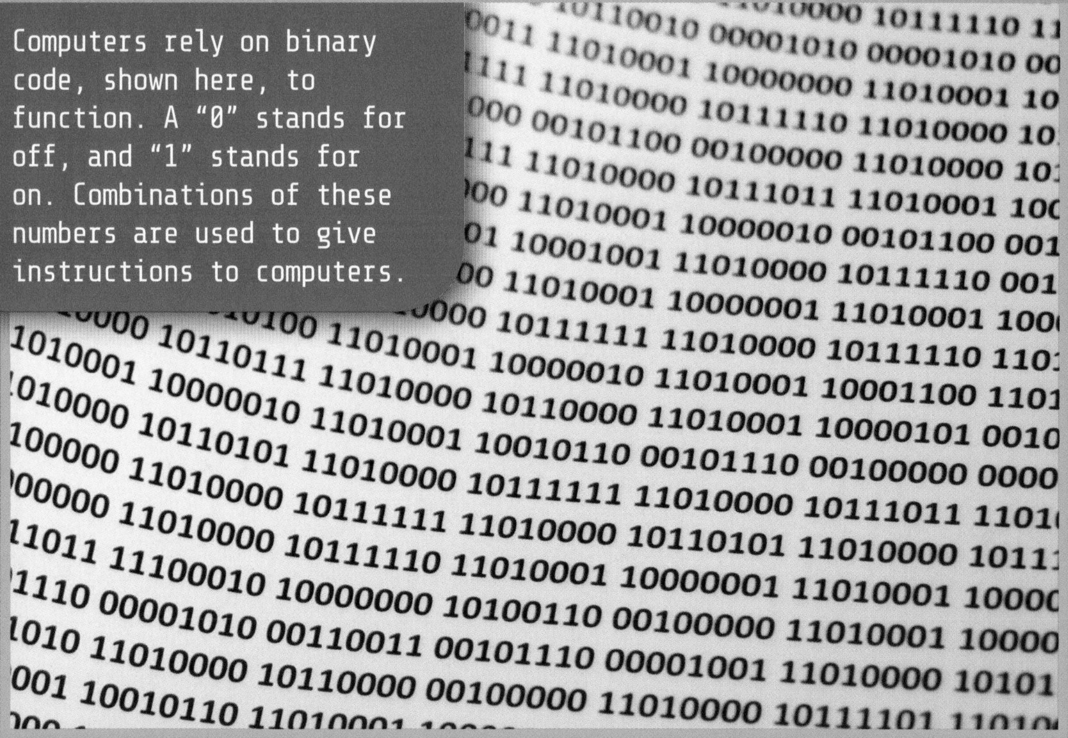

```
0011 11010010 00001010 00001010 00
1111 11010001 10000000 11010001 10
000 00101100 00100000 11010000 10
111 11010000 10111011 11010001 100
01 10001001 11010000 10111110 001
000 10111111 11010000 10111110 110
10000010 11010001 10001100 1101
11010001 10000101 0010
00101110 00100000 0000
11010000 10111011 1101
11010000 1011
11010001 10000
11010001 10000
11010000 10101
11010000 10111101 1101
```

XOR gate

A ——⟩⟩D—— Output
B ——

A	B	Output
0	0	0
0	1	1
1	0	1
1	1	0

Truth Tables

This picture introduces the concept of truth tables. Coders understand how their gates work by using truth tables. Truth tables show all the possible inputs and shows outputs based on the math connected to a gate. The truth table for the XOR gate is shown in the diagram. Can you make truth tables for the other gates in this book?

Don't Forget Your Umbrella!

Computers complete complex tasks using Boolean logic. Digital **integrated** circuits pack many gates into a very small space. As technology improves, even more gates will be used in the same space.

Here's a simple quiz of your understanding of gates. Name the gate and if the output is "true" ("on"), or "false" ("off").

Do you take your umbrella?
Only if the output is true!

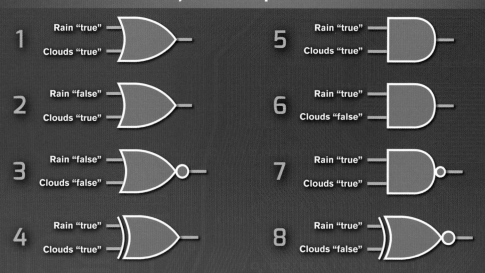

KEY
1) OR true 2) OR false 3) NOR true 4) XOR false 5) AND true 6) AND false 7) NAND false 8) XNOR false

Glossary

circuit: The complete path that an electrical current travels along.

complex: Having many parts.

component: A part of a larger whole.

diode: An electronic device that allows an electric current to flow in one direction only.

exclusive: Having the power to keep something out; limited.

integrated: Having various parts linked together.

logic: The science that studies the formal processes used in thinking and reasoning.

master's thesis: A long paper written on a subject to earn a master's college degree.

mechanical: Having to do with machinery.

microprocessor: A part of a computer that controls what the computer does.

probability: The chance that something will happen.

relay: An electronically operated switch.

schematic: The main parts of something shown as a drawing or diagram.

transistor: A small device used to control the flow of electricity in computers and other electronic devices.

Index

Websites

Due to the changing nature of Internet links, PowerKids Press has developed an online list of websites related to the subject of this book. This site is updated regularly. Please use this link to access the list: www.powerkidslinks.com/kcc/bool